Tiptoes and Fin
by
Brian Ogder
Illustrated by Simon Smith

Hi! My name's Brian and I've really enjoyed getting mixed up with the **Livewires**. What a bunch! Come with us as **Boot**, the computer, takes us on strange adventures in strange places. Hang on to your hair, grab your shades and we're off... Talking of shades, **Tempo** has just nudged me and said it's **Digit's** turn now.

Text copyright © Brian Ogder 1997

Illustrations copyright © Simon Smith 1997

The author asserts the moral right to be identified as the author of this work.

Published by
The Bible Reading Fellowship
Peter's Way, Sandy Lane West
Oxford OX4 5HG
ISBN 0 7459 3523 0
Albatross Books Pty Ltd
PO Box 320, Sutherland
NSW 2232, Australia
ISBN 0 7324 1565 9

First edition 1997

10 9 8 7 6 5 4 3 2 1 0

All rights reserved

Acknowledgments
Unless otherwise stated, scripture quotations are taken from the Good News Bible published by The Bible Societies/ HarperCollins Publishers Ltd UK © American Bible Society, 1966, 1971, 1976, 1992.

A catalogue record for this book is available from the British Library.

Printed and bound in Malta by Interprint Limited

An imprint of
The Bible Reading Fellowship

Greetings, folks!

The trouble with authors is they do get in the way sometimes. Now let me tell you what's really going on 'cos you may not have caught up with us before. You see, we're a really cool bunch. There's Annie-log—she's the one in the pic with the computer. Then there's her sister—Data. Tim is the one who looks like a haystack and he sort of takes care of Tempo (or is it the other way round?). You can tell them apart 'cos Tempo's got four legs.

David, the shepherd king, lived from about 1000 BC until 961 BC, in the country we now call Israel. His home was Bethlehem, the same town where a thousand years later Jesus was born. David wrote many Psalms and was a skilled soldier and harp player.

Praise God in his Temple! Praise his strength in heaven! Praise him for the mighty things he has done. Praise his supreme greatness. Praise him with trumpets. Praise him with harps and lyres. Praise him with drums and dancing. Praise him with harps and flutes. Praise him with cymbals. Praise him with loud cymbals. Praise the Lord, all living creatures! Praise the Lord!

PSALM 150

There are eleven words from the Psalm in the wordsearch. Cross off David's sheep as you find them.

```
S T E P M U R T
U B H M C T C S
P R A I S E Y E
R L R G L M M T
E O P H Y P B U
M R S T R L A L
E D F Y E E L F
D R U M S D S E
```

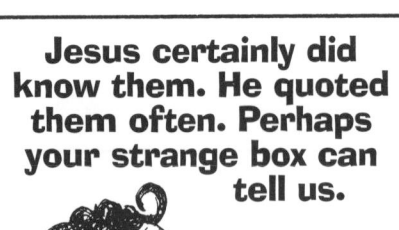

Little Ben is the youngest of the gang. Then there's Boot, Annie-log's computer, who comes everywhere with us. Not to forget Tychi—the mouse with the longest tail in history. Oh, I nearly forgot, there's my sister Quartz—she's always dancing about. I'm Digit—rhymes with fidget, which is what Quartz should really be called ! You won't see me without my sketch pad! One day we were having a natter about music...

Boot ↓

Tychi
Tyki
Tichy
Tick
↙

What about that new pop group then? You know, The Blurbs.

No way—the classics are best—Mozart and Beethoven.

Boot, can you tell us what sort of music there was in the Bible?

I like Bach.

I can play the mouse organ.

Boot whirred and spluttered and the Livewires found themselves being whisked into his disk drive.

The Livewires joined in as David sang some more. Data soon got the hang of playing the harp.
Boot's multi-media speakers joined with the harps that David and Data were playing.

No speech or words are used, no sound is heard; yet their message goes out to all the world and is heard to the ends of the earth. God made a home in the sky for the sun; it comes out in the morning like a happy bridegroom, like an athlete eager to run a race. It starts at one end of the sky and goes across to the other. Nothing can hide from its heat.

PSALM 19.3-6

That was great. I usually only have the sheep joining in! By the way, do keep the harp. It'll remind you to sing God's praise.

Fantastic... I mean, thanks, DAVE.

David sang 'how clearly the sky reveals God's glory'.

Heavenly Father, help us to see your glory and your greatness in the world about us—in a tiny insect or a beautiful sunset.

Try this harp quiz. It is based on the verses from Psalm 19. Apart from the first word all the others go down the harp—not across it.

Across:
'Each night ...... it to the next.'

Down:
1. Means 'shows'.
2. .... day announces it.
3. We sing God's ......
4. Another word for world
5. A runner is an '.....'
6. Eager .. run a race.
7. No '......' or words are used.

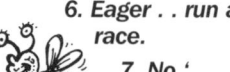

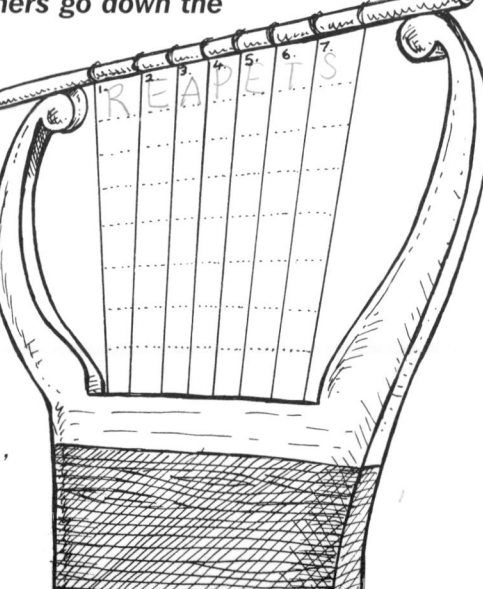

DIARY

SUNDAY
David lived in Bethlehem. Who was born in Bethlehem a thousand years later?

MONDAY
Can you play a musical instrument? If not, why not learn to play one!

TUESDAY
David thought that God was like a shepherd who cares for his sheep. How would you describe God? One person thought he is like a pilot, flying a plane safely and caring for the passengers.

WEDNESDAY
David played a harp called a kinnor. How many different musical instruments can you find in Psalm 150?

THURSDAY
Dear God, thank you for giving us voices to sing and bodies to dance.

FRIDAY
Can you remember the verse you learned from the Psalms? If so, then write it down here...

SATURDAY
This book is called Tiptoes and Fingertips—we stretch up towards God and we stretch out in faith and find him all around us. Can you do some stretching exercises: up on your toes with your arms in the air—how high can you reach? And then arms out at your sides reaching out as far as they will go.

Suddenly Boot began to whirr and wheeze.

PSALM 100:4 — "Enter the temple gates with thanksgiving, go into its courts with praise. Give thanks to him and praise him."

Where is the Temple, Boot?

And the LIVEWIRES were whisked once again into Boot's disk drive.

They had swopped the quiet countryside near Bethlehem for the bustle and noise of a large city. Boot gave them the answer to Annie-log's question.

And now we are here, standing inside the gates of Jerusalem!

PSALM 122:2

Annie-log typed a request for a map.

ISRAEL
Jerusalem
Bethlehem

Can you unscramble some of the fruit and vegetables for sale in Jerusalem? There were people everywhere.

VOILES
GIFS
TEADS
PRAGES
NOONIS
SKEEL
SAPE

The Livewires had to keep jumping out of the way as loaded donkeys trotted by. Shop keepers were shouting, customers arguing, armed soldiers pushing their way through the crowds. The city, which seemed to be built on a number of small hills, had some fine large buildings. The Livewires were just beginning to wonder what to do when they heard a familiar voice from behind...

11

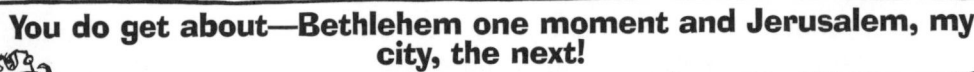

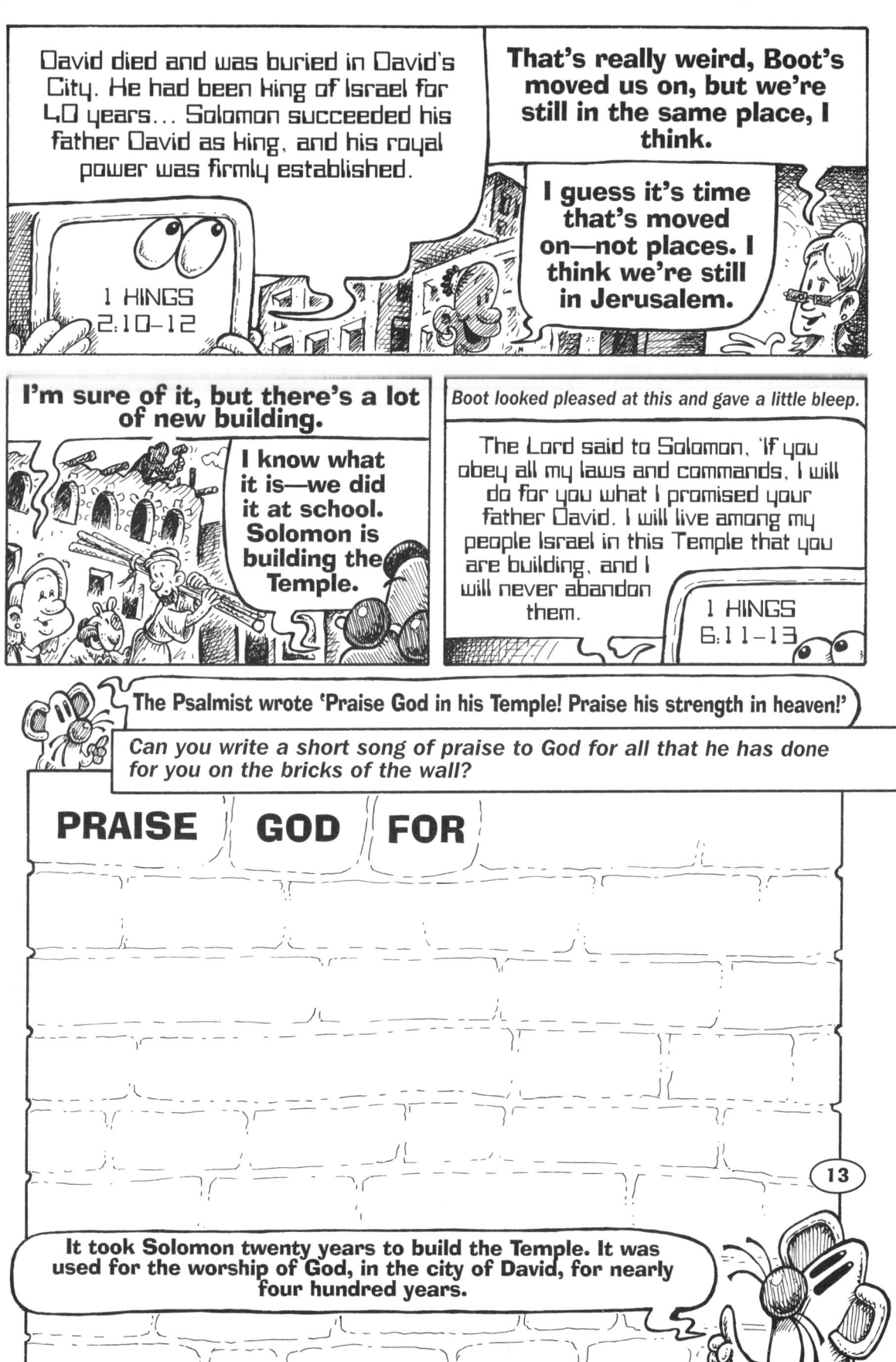

Even as the Livewires were watching, the city wall began to crumble and fall in front of them. Boot whirred and whizzed and as the wall fell the Livewires were caught up in a whirl of dust and whisked into the computer. As the dust settled around them they saw a new verse on Boot's screen.

In 596 BC Nebuzaradan burnt down the Temple, the palace, and the houses of all the important people in Jerusalem, and his soldiers tore down the city walls.

2 KINGS 25:9

I don't like this—it's really scary.

I think it's like last time—we've moved in time, but we're still in Jerusalem.

It sure doesn't look the same. Let's ask this guy.

It was terrible when the Babylonians came.

The Babylonians attacked Jerusalem and destroyed the city.

They took away to Babylon all the skilled workmen. They left only the poorest people to work in the vineyards and fields.

Lord, help us, even in the darkest moments, to remember that you are there with us.

They took away everything that was made of gold or silver.

The old man was looking very sad. The Livewires thought it might cheer him up if you coloured the picture.

(14)

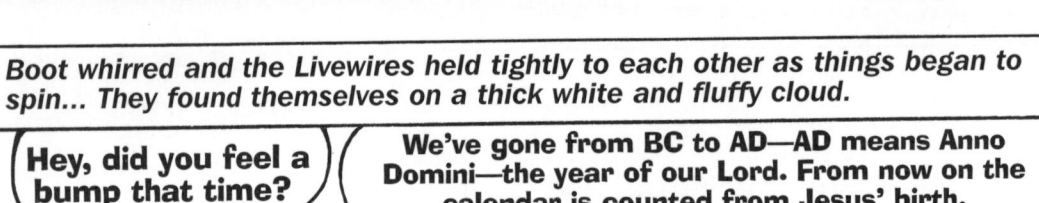

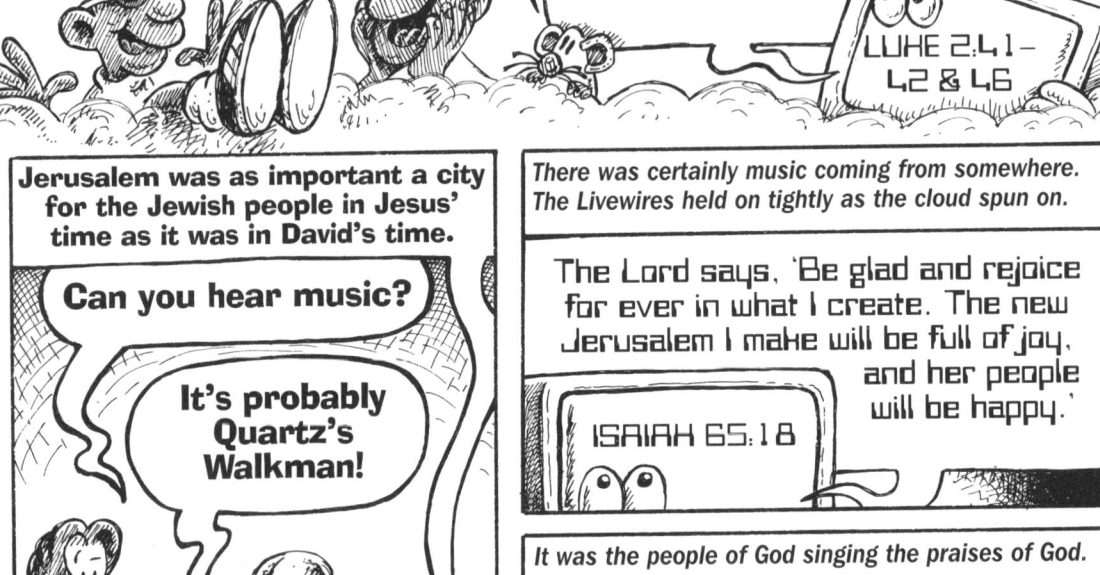

DIARY

SUNDAY
Imagine you were going on holiday to Israel today. What would you like to see most?

MONDAY
Can you fill in the missing vowels in these words?

Z _ _ N   J _ R _ S _ L _ M   D _ V _ D   J _ B _ S T _ S

TUESDAY
These words have become joined together. Put a line between them.
ThepsalmistwrotepraiseGodinhistemplepraisehisstrengthinheaven.

WEDNESDAY
Think about someone who is having a really hard time at the moment—and then pray for them. It might be a friend or it might even be a whole country.

THURSDAY
Imagine you had to leave home and live in a foreign country. What would you miss most?

FRIDAY

> Heavenly Father, you want only what is best for us. Help me to make your world a better place for everyone to live in.

SATURDAY
Digit has written this message in code. Can you crack the code? heyt oundf esusJ ni het empleT. Boot decided it was time to move on. The cloud suddenly stopped spinning and the Livewires found themselves falling through its fluffy whiteness...

They fell in a heap in what seemed to be a large city.

People were pushing past them, busy market stalls were selling fruit and vegetables, and in the distance they saw soldiers.

This is Jerusalem in the year AD 30.

As the Livewires picked themselves up a man walked towards them. It was Peter, one of the friends of Jesus. He stopped to speak to them.

Excuse me, but have you seen a crowd of people? I'm trying to find Jesus and there's always a lot of people with him.

I'm sorry but we've only just got here. We would like to find Jesus too.

Follow me then, and I'll tell you about him.

Come with me, and I will teach you to catch people.

MATTHEW 4:19

Data read out the verse that Boot had found.

That's really strange. Those were the words Jesus spoke to me when he called me to follow him.

Yes, we know. We did it at school.

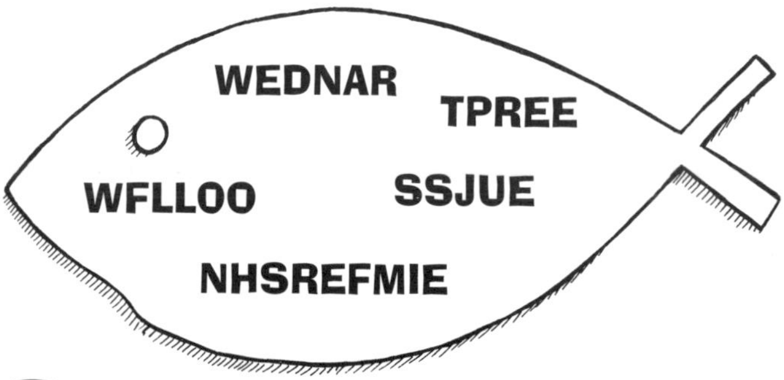

WEDNAR TPREE
WFLLOO SSJUE
NHSREFMIE

Try to make sense of these sentences by unscrambling the words.

_ _ _ _ _ and his brother
_ _ _ _ _ _ were
_ _ _ _ _ _ _ _ _ when
_ _ _ _ _ called them to
_ _ _ _ _ _ him.

18

LUKE 13:20

The Kingdom of God is like this. A woman takes some yeast and mixes it with forty litres of flour until the whole batch of dough rises.

That's another story Jesus told about the kingdom of God. The yeast is only small but it makes all the difference to the whole loaf. Jesus told some wonderful stories about the kingdom. They were simple stories about everyday things.

250ml water, teaspoon sugar, 25gm butter, 400gm flour, 1/2 teaspoon salt, 7gm dried yeast.

Warm the water, mix the sugar with the water and add the yeast. Leave in a warm place. Rub the butter into the flour and salt. Put a small amount into a dish, cover it, and put it on one side. Add the yeast mixture to the rest and mix into a dough. Leave covered. WATCH WHAT HAPPENS! In an hour knead the mixture. Put into two bread tins, leave for 20 minutes and bake for 25 minutes in an oven at 220°C. After an hour was there any difference between the small amount in the dish and the rest?

Heavenly Father, help us to show others your kingdom by the way we live our lives, speak to people and show that we care.

All this time the Livewires had been walking through the streets of Jerusalem with Peter as he told them about Jesus and the kingdom of God. As they turned a corner they suddenly saw in front of them a group of Roman soldiers. This picture would look great if you coloured it. A very tall Roman soldier, carrying a spear, came over to them.

Keep that animal under control or there will be trouble.

My young friend didn't mean any harm.

I'm sorry, sir.

A lot of people think that when Jesus talks about the kingdom of God he means he will drive the Romans out of the country and become king. But this is not what he has come for. His kingdom is not one where soldiers fight and kill. It is one where ordinary people like you and me love God and love our neighbours too.

The soldier returned to his friends. Peter explained to the Livewires that Israel was occupied by the Romans. They had to do what the Romans wanted. The country was not really their own. Most people hated having the Romans ruling them.

Boot had been listening carefully to what Peter was saying. He gave a little bleep.

Father, we pray for all countries where people are ruled by soldiers and cannot say or do what they want.

My kingdom does not belong to this world; if my kingdom belonged to this world, my followers would fight to keep me from being handed over to the Jewish authorities.

JOHN 18:36

DIARY

SUNDAY
Pray today for all those who go to other countries to tell people about the kingdom of God.

MONDAY
Look at the parable of the sower again. Colour the picture as you think about it.

TUESDAY
Check how your mustard and cress are growing. Do they need any water?

WEDNESDAY
Plan to buy the ingredients and get a grown-up to help you make some bread.

THURSDAY
Can you think of any countries where people are not free to say and do what they want? You might like to pray for them.

FRIDAY
Can you think of any signs that people use to show that they are Christians?

SATURDAY
Father, thank you for all that Jesus taught about your kingdom. Thank you that I can be in your kingdom. Help me to tell others about it.

Farewell... for now!

Did you know that the story of Palm Sunday actually starts with a password? Jesus sent two of his friends ahead of the rest of the group to get the transport he wanted. He gave them a secret password.

'Go to the village there ahead of you; as you go in, you will find a colt tied up that has never been ridden. Untie it and bring it here. If someone asks you why you are untying it, tell him that the Master needs it.'

LUKE 19.28–35

The disciples went on their way and found everything just as Jesus had told them.

As they were untying the colt, its owner said to them, 'Why are you untying it?'

'The Master needs it,' they answered.

And they took the colt to Jesus.

Why not colour in Digit's sketch?

Heavenly Father, the owner of the colt gave his donkey to Jesus willingly. Help us to give our things for you.

After Peter left them the Livewires walked around the city of Jerusalem. It seemed to be very crowded, rather like a big town at home just before Christmas. After an hour or so the Livewires decided to leave the city and try and find somewhere quiet. But before they had gone very far they found themselves in the middle of a crowd again.

Peter said that the crowds follow Jesus. Do you think he is here?

I think today must be what is called Palm Sunday. You know, the day Jesus rode into Jerusalem on a donkey.

Yes, I remember...

Don't tell us, you did it at school!

Tempo was getting very excited by the crowd and the Livewires stood on their tiptoes trying to see over the heads of the people.

When Jesus came near Jerusalem, the large crowd of his disciples began to thank God and praise him in loud voices for all the great things that they had seen.

LUKE 19:37

Boot has muddled things up. Can you sort out what the crowd were shouting?

Godsselbthegnikwhosemocin ehtnamefothedroL! Peaceniheavendnagloryotgod!

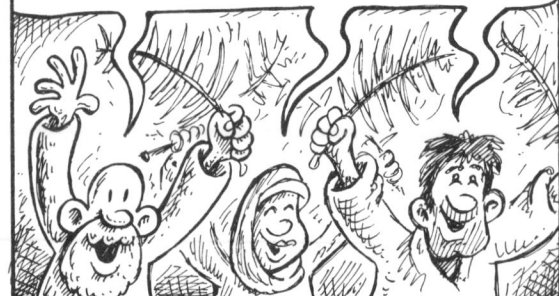

26

The Livewires were so busy trying to see over the crowd that they didn't notice Peter coming up behind them.

"May your holy name be honoured."

"er... may your kingdom come."

"What a wonderful day it has been. All these people coming out to cheer Jesus as he rides into Jerusalem."

"But he rode on a donkey. You'd think a king would ride on a horse."

"A king who comes in peace always rides on a donkey. Only a king who comes for war rides a horse. Don't they do that in your country?"

"Well, no, not really. So Jesus is the King of Peace?"

Shout for joy, you people of Jerusalem! Look, your king is coming to you! He comes triumphant and victorious, but humble and riding on a donkey.

ZECHARIAH 9:9

"Your clever square friend has reminded me. It was Zechariah, one of our prophets, who told us that our king would come in peace."

"Time to exercise, everyone! Stretch high on your tiptoes and wave your hands. That's how everyone is greeting Jesus."

Do not let your hands hang limp!

ZEPHANIAH 3:16

Can you unscramble some of the special days we have around Easter?

A SANDY PLUM

STAY A REED

DODGY FAIRO

Heavenly Father, thank you that Jesus came as King of Peace. May he bring peace to our world again.

(27)

Boot spluttered and whirred and the Livewires found things beginning to spin again. They landed in the Temple Court. It was a large paved area. There were tables set out and people were exchanging money and selling pigeons. All of these were for use in the Temple. It was very noisy and crowded. It seemed that something rather strange had just happened. There was money and pigeons everywhere!

Jerusalem was really crowded because it was festival time. The Passover was very special for the Jewish people. It was the time they remembered when God helped them escape from being slaves in Egypt and spared their first-born children. Hundreds of Jewish people always went to the Temple in Jerusalem during the Passover.

Jesus went into the Temple and drove out all those who were buying and selling there. He overturned the tables of the moneychangers and the stools of those who sold pigeons.

MATTHEW 21:12

How many pigeons can you count?

The dust and feathers slowly settled and the Livewires spotted Peter coming towards them.

May your holy name be honoured.

May your kingdom come. My friends, I am glad I've seen you. It is getting dangerous to be seen as a follower of Jesus. I think you should leave Jerusalem quickly before the Temple guard catch you.

But we haven't done anything wrong.

We all have as far as the priests are concerned. We believe that Jesus is someone very special. They don't like that. Now, quickly, out of the Temple. I will find you again soon. May God take care of you.

The Livewires looked at each and ran towards the gate of the city with Tempo barking behind them.

"That was scary. All those crowds of people and the Temple guards."

"It isn't very easy being a follower of Jesus, is it? Peter and his friends are very brave."

"I bet Tempo would keep them off."

"Look, it's Peter again."

"Growl."

The Livewires and Peter exchanged the passwords as before. Peter sat down with them.

"Praise God you got away safely. Jesus has really stirred up the priests this time. You see, the Temple makes a profit from the money-changers who sell the only coins allowed to be used in the Temple. It also makes money from those men who sell the pigeons. The pigeons are sold to poor visitors who can't afford more. They give them to the priests as an offering."

"So when Jesus let all those pigeons fly away and tipped all the money on the floor it really upset the Temple priests—I can understand that."

"It sort of looked a bit like a supermarket before!"

Jesus said, 'My Temple will be called a house of prayer. But you are making it a hideout for thieves.'

MATTHEW 21:13

This would be a great time to learn the passwords the Livewires used: 'May your holy name be honoured. May your kingdom come.'

Heavenly Father, help us to find both a time and a place where we can be quiet with you every day.

Can you find some words you have learnt in this wordsearch?

```
O A D T F H J C
P R I E S T U Z
E Y V M A Y T P
H O L Y F E S X
G U F D B C N B
H R J K E L A M
T R S Q P O M N
U P R A I S E D
```

coo!

Peter sat with the Livewires for a while under the shade of the palms, thinking about all that happened when Jesus came to Jerusalem.

The blind and the crippled came to him in the Temple, and he healed them.

The chief priests and the teachers of the Law became angry when they saw the wonderful things Jesus was doing.

MATTHEW 21:15

I don't think things are going so well for Jesus.

You could be right.

They didn't like the fact that the children were shouting in the Temple, 'Praise to David's son!'

Well, I would have done the same.

Data pulled out her little harp and began plucking at its strings. Soon everyone was joining in.

O Lord, our Lord, your greatness is seen in all the world! Your praise reaches up to the heavens; it is sung by children and babies.

Heavenly Father, help me to praise you even when things seem to be going wrong.

PSALM 8:1-2

It was the song that David had taught them.

DIARY

SUNDAY
Can you think of something of yours which God might want to use? It might be something you can do—something you are good at.

MONDAY
What makes you cheer? Is it when something good happens or a sports result or when you see someone you think a lot of?

TUESDAY
Write down the reply to the passwords Peter taught the Livewires—'May your name be honoured. May...'

WEDNESDAY
Many people say that churches have a special feeling to them. People have worshipped God in some churches for hundreds of years. How do you feel when you go into a church?

THURSDAY
Can you think of some Bible stories where the followers of Jesus were very brave? Some Christians have to be very brave today.

FRIDAY
Did you make up a tune to the Bible verse you learnt?

SATURDAY

> Heavenly Father, thank you for the courage Jesus had in going on with his work when people were against him. Help me to stand up for you.

Peter sat with the Livewires a little longer. Their singing seemed to have done him good. Finally, he jumped to his feet and started back towards the city. Then a thought came to him and, turning back, he put something into Annie-log's hand before waving goodbye and setting off down the hill. It was a flat clay tablet, with a simple map of Jerusalem to help them to find their way about. The tablet looked like this. The map gives the first letter of some of the names but it needs you to finish them off.

Temple

High Priest's House

Golgotha

Garden of Gethsemane

Antonia Fortress

Herod's Palace

Jesus said, 'I must go to Jerusalem and suffer much from the elders, the chief priests, and the teachers of the Law. I will be put to death, but three days later I will be raised to life.'

MATTHEW 16:21

Father, thank you for the courage of Jesus in going to Jerusalem knowing what was going to happen. Help us to face difficulties with courage.

The Livewires looked at the figure of Peter getting smaller and smaller as he walked away from them. Suddenly they felt quite sad and lonely. The sun seemed to have gone behind a cloud. Even Tempo seemed to feel the sadness. He lay quietly with his head on his paws and whined softly to himself. Boot gave a little sigh and bleeped quietly.

The Livewires had dozed off in the quietness. They woke up with a start to find Boot whirring and buzzing and they were drawn once again into his disk drive. Data only just had time to grab hold of her harp as they whirled through the air. As everything settled they found themselves half way up a small hill. There seemed to be gardens laid out on the hillside. Peter was coming towards them. He looked around as though someone might be following him. He seemed to be very worried.

May your holy name be honoured.

May your kingdom come. Though I don't think it will now.

Peter, whatever is the matter? What's wrong?

It's the end of everything, everything we had counted on. Jesus is dead. His followers have scattered all over the city. I came back here because this was always a special place for Jesus.

Can you tell us what happened, please?

It all started with a special meal we had with Jesus. It was the last supper he was going to eat with us, he said.

He insisted on washing our . . . . just like a servant would.

He took a piece of . . . . . , broke it, and gave it to us.

Jesus took a . . . , gave thanks to God, and said, 'Take this and share it among yourselves.'

During the meal Jesus said, 'I tell you, one of you will betray me.'

Can you fill in the missing words?

PCU   ETEF   ADBER

After the supper we still didn't realize what was going to happen. At the end of the meal Jesus said something I just couldn't believe. He told me that I would tell others I didn't know him, that I would deny him. He was right! I can hardly bear to think about it. Jesus always loved this garden and so it wasn't really a surprise when he told us that he wanted to come here to pray. It was quite late and some of us were very tired.

Then Jesus went with his disciples to a place called Gethsemane, and he said to them, 'Sit here while I go over there and pray.'

MATTHEW 26:36

Jesus threw himself on the ground and prayed.

He returned to the three of us but found us asleep.

Judas came with a large crowd. 'The man I kiss is the man you want,' he said. Then we all left him and ran away.

Jesus, you must have felt very lonely in the garden when your friends fell asleep. Please be close to us at times of loneliness.

Can you sort out the names of the disciples whom Jesus took with him to pray?

RETEP   MJSAE   NHJO

34

Peter put his head in his hands. 'It was awful,' he said. 'The Lord turned round and looked straight at me and then I remembered what he had said: Before the cock crows tonight, you will say three times that you do not know me.' Peter wept bitterly at the memory. The Livewires sat quietly beside him. A large tear rolled down Data's cheek.

Although it felt rather creepy in the dark on the Mount of Olives, with Tempo barking from time to time at strange noises, the Livewires badly wanted to know what happened next.

So Jesus was tried by the High Priests—but what for? Surely he hadn't done anything wrong?

But the priests wanted him out of the way. He was more popular than they were. So they made up a lie and they took him to Pontius Pilate, the Roman Governor.

Remember that the Romans ruled Israel at this time. The Jews were not allowed to put people to death. Only the Roman governor could give the orders.

LUKE 23:13-21

Pilate said, 'I have not found him guilty... so I will let him go. The whole crowd cried out, 'Kill him!'

Jesus, people told lies to have you put to death. Help us always to tell the truth.

Pilate wanted to set Jesus free, so he appealed to the crowd again. But they shouted back, 'Crucify him! Crucify him!'

The priests told Pilate that Jesus had called himself the King of the _ _ _ _. But Jesus had always said that his kingdom was the Kingdom of _ _ _.

Tempo started to bark loudly—Tim did his best to quieten him. Peter and the Livewires hid in the bushes as they heard footsteps coming towards them. They could just see the figure of a young man walking up the hill. When he got closer Peter called out to him.

May your holy name be honoured.

May your kingdom come.

A certain young man was following Jesus. They tried to arrest him, but he ran away.

MARK 14:51

Peter introduced Mark, a close friend, to the surprised Livewires. Between them, Peter and Mark told them the rest of the sad story.

Jesus had to carry his cross through the city of Jerusalem

The Roman soldiers played dice for his coat.

Two criminals were crucified next to Jesus.

At three o'clock Jesus died.

The Roman officer said, 'This was really the Son of God.'

Peter and Mark were crying by the time they had finished the story. The Livewires too were close to tears. It all seemed so final.

We may not know, we cannot tell what pains he had to bear, But we believe it was for us he hung and suffered there.

DIARY

SUNDAY
Have a look at the map Peter gave the Livewires. Can you see where all the events of the week took place? You could make a larger version and write in what happened.

MONDAY
We remember Jesus' last supper in church. It is sometimes called Holy Communion.

TUESDAY
Think of anyone you know who is lonely. Perhaps you could make friends with someone like that at school?

WEDNESDAY
It isn't always easy to tell people that you follow Jesus. Remember God always hears and answers prayers—even quick ones.

THURSDAY
Today is Thursday. On Maundy Thursday the Queen meets a group of older people and gives them Maundy money. Can you find out any more about this custom?

FRIDAY
Good Friday may have got its name from God's Friday: the day we remember Jesus being crucified. Look at those pictures again and think about the story.

SATURDAY

> Heavenly Father, thank you that the love which Jesus has for us took him to the cross. Help us to love you in return.

Boot rumbled and whirred and drew the Livewires into his disk drive. They tumbled out again, still in the dark, but on another hillside.

Early on Sunday morning, while it was still dark, Mary Magdalene went to the tomb and saw that the stone had been taken away from the entrance.

JOHN 20:1

This place is a bit spooky, all those caves and things.

I wondor if there are any rabbits?

Sh... I think there's someone coming.

I hope it's not the soldiers again.

Just in front of them a woman came running up to one of the caves. She looked at it and then ran off again. Half an hour later two men came running up. One of them was Peter. Although he got there last he went straight into the cave. He came out shouting and smiling. It was lighter now and he saw the Livewires and came over.

Praise the Lord! I can hardly believe it but Jesus isn't dead—he's alive.

But you were so sure it was the end yesterday. What's happened? What's changed?

Mary, one of Jesus' friends came and found John and me. She had come to the tomb where he was buried. There was a big rock put in front so we couldn't steal him away and say he was alive. Mary found the rock had gone and she came and got us. John always did run faster than me. But this means that Jesus was right. He has come alive again. I must go and tell the others.

Can you think of some words which describe how Peter felt when he found Jesus was alive? Here are some Boot has mixed up again for you.

ZAMEAD   ZEADD   SHEDASTONI   PPYHA   LIGHTDEED

Mary stood crying outside the tomb.

JOHN 20:11

Peter left the Livewires. A few moments later they saw Mary come back again. This time she looked in to the cave. As she was doing this the Livewires saw the figure of a man come up to Mary. Minutes later Mary walked towards them. She, like Peter, had a big smile on her face. Just as she was walking past the Livewires, Data spoke to her.

Yes, it's truly wonderful. I've just spoken to Jesus! He is alive! I thought he must have been the gardener who took the body away. But it wasn't—it was Jesus.

Excuse me, but you see we're friends of Peter. Could you please tell us what has happened?

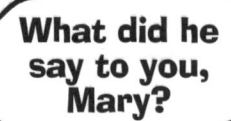

What did he say to you, Mary?

He asked me why I was crying and who I was looking for. Then he just spoke my name. He just said 'Mary'. I wanted to stay with him, but he told me I must go and tell the others. I really must go now—they'll be so excited.

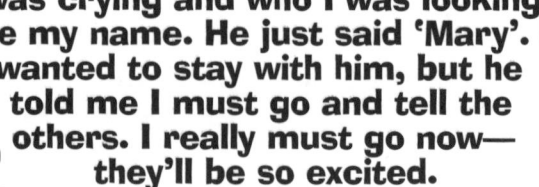

Heavenly Father, thank you that Jesus came alive again and that we can know him and love him today.

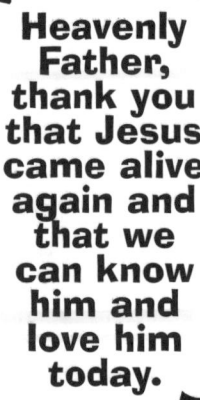

Just a thought, but you may not know that caves outside Jerusalem were often made into tombs. This one had been given for Jesus by Joseph from Arimathea. A heavy stone was put in front to seal it.

DIARY

SUNDAY
Did you sort out the words that described how Peter might have felt? AMAZED, DAZED, ASTONISHED, HAPPY and DELIGHTED. Think of another word to describe how you might have felt.

MONDAY
Can you think of anyone who is unhappy at the moment? Ask God to be very close to them.

TUESDAY
Easter would be a good time to have a party to celebrate Jesus' resurrection.

WEDNESDAY
Abandon the telly! Go for a walk! Stretch your fingers and toes!

THURSDAY
The fishermen, the lake, the dawn and the fire on the beach would make a great picture.

FRIDAY
Write out that short verse you learned—check that you know it.

SATURDAY

Look at all the prayers printed for this week. Think about them and use them again.

Peter and the Livewires were sitting in their favourite spot on the Mount of Olives, just outside Jerusalem. Data was playing her harp and humming quietly to herself. Tempo had barked at some rabbits so Tim had taken him for a run. They both lay panting in the shade of an old tree.

It's good to get out of the city for some fresh air. No wonder Jesus loved this place. Of course the grave that Joseph lent him is just over there.

I've been wondering about that. Wasn't Joseph, of somewhere I can't say properly, a Jewish leader?

Peter laughed. 'Arimathea—a village on the west side of the city', he said. 'Yes, he was. There were several secret followers of Jesus—two of them members of the Sanhedrin'.

You seem to have a lot of secrets. What with passwords and now secret followers, it's really exciting.

er ... 'scuse me but what's the Sanhedthing?

Sanhedrin means 'Council'. (There are seventy members of the Sanhedrin, plus the High Priest.) It's made up of the most important Jewish leaders. It's a sort of Jewish government. The Sanhedrin runs most things in the country—only a few have to be decided by the Romans.

Who were the secret followers of Jesus?

If you like, I'll ask one of them if you can meet him tomorrow.

Will it be safe? Can we trust him?

I'm sure you can. His name is Nicodemus. Remember the password though.

Can you remember the password?

The next day, as Peter had promised them, they saw a stranger climbing up the hill towards them.

May your kingdom come.

Thank you, sir, for coming. We know you are a very busy and important man. Peter told us you are now a follower of Jesus.

Nicodemus looked rather nervously around as though expecting to have been followed up the hill.

Yes, I have been a secret follower of Jesus. Like a lot of people I heard about him first when he did some miracles. One dark night, so dark that no one could recognize me, I went to see him. I told him that I knew he was a teacher sent by God. He told me that I must be born again.

'How can a grown man be born again?' Nicodemus asked. Jesus replied, 'No one can enter the Kingdom of God without being born of water and the Spirit.'

JOHN 3.4-5

For God loved the world so much that he gave his only Son, so that everyone who believes in him may not die but have eternal life.

JOHN 3.16

Jesus spoke to me and I was sure that he was right. He was telling the truth in a way that our religious leaders were not doing. I became a follower then. But it was not easy being a member of the Sanhedrin and I had to keep Jesus as a secret.

Get a highlighter or a felt pen and find the name of some of the followers of Jesus in this word search. The names go backwards as well as forwards. There are seven names.

**NMSSEMAJJKMNPETERANSFLPQRNICODEMUSFREDANDGRE
DANDREWWEDRTYHPESOJDKILETJOHNYRAMDREMZ**

Sometime later I had the opportunity to speak up for Jesus to the Sanhedrin.

That must have been very brave of you.

It wasn't much, but I had to do something! It happened like this. Jesus spoke in the temple. He made the Council very cross with what he said. They sent guards to arrest him, but the guards were so impressed by Jesus that they didn't lay a hand on him.

'Whoever is thirsty should come to me, and whoever believes in me should drink.'

Yes, that's what he said—it reminded me of what he had said to me about being born of water and the Spirit. It was at the meeting of the Sanhedrin Council afterwards. The others were telling off the guards for not arresting Jesus. I just reminded them that we didn't judge anyone until we had heard them. Some of the others, I'm sure, began to get suspicious of me then.

JOHN 7:37

Heavenly Father, there are many times when we can only do little things for you. Give us the courage to do them.

In your diary or on a piece of paper write down some of the little things you could do for God. It might mean talking with someone you don't really like. It might mean doing a job at home you aren't keen on. It might just mean keeping your bedroom tidy.

DIARY

SUNDAY
Pray today for all those who are secret followers of Jesus throughout the world—for whatever reason they may have.

MONDAY
John 3:16 is one of the most famous verses in the Bible. It would be a very good verse to learn by heart.

TUESDAY
Have another look at the list of little things you might do for God. Is there anything you can add to it? Praying for other people might be one.

WEDNESDAY
Making decisions can sometimes be quite hard. You can chat it over with your mum or dad or talk to your best friend. Don't forget to ask God as well.

THURSDAY
Can you think of some words that would describe Peter? He was...

FRIDAY
Tempo says his brain is spinning with all the info. Could you draw a large picture of Tempo looking like that?

SATURDAY

> Heavenly Father, thank you for this past week, for all that I have done and learnt. I pray for the days ahead, that you will be near me and I will be near you.

Boot whirred and chugged. He gave a long bleep and stretched himself. The whirring got louder and the Livewires were drawn, once again, into his disk drive.

They spent their time in learning from the apostles, taking part in the fellowship, and sharing in the fellowship meals and the prayers.

ACTS 2:42

They seemed to have landed in the middle of a crowd of people. In front of the crowd was a face they recognized. It was Peter. Tempo jumped up when he saw Peter. Peter scratched his head.

It is good to see you all again. No need for a password this time. Isn't it wonderful to see so many people longing to hear more about Jesus?

What's been happening since we saw you last?

The Holy Spirit came just as Jesus had promised. All these people have become followers and we are trying hard to teach them all. They are so keen, so enthusiastic, to follow Jesus. We eat together and pray together and best of all we worship together.

There's a group over there bringing all sorts of bits and pieces.

Yes, everyone is sharing all they have—clothes and furniture and money. All for the Lord.

What Peter didn't say was that he spoke in Jerusalem after the Holy Spirit had come to the disciples. As a result of what he said over 3,000 people started to follow Jesus. Just amazing! It was these folk that Peter and the others were trying to teach.

Father, I pray for all those who teach others about you—for ministers, for missionaries and for teachers in school and church.

Is there something that you can give to God? It might be half an hour each week visiting an older person or someone who can't get out much. Think about it.

53

The members of the Council threw Stephen out of the city and stoned him. The witnesses left their cloaks in the care of a young man named Saul.

ACTS 7:57-58

It was a very sad day for all of us. Stephen was the first of us to die because he believed in Jesus. There have been many more since.

Dear Lord Jesus, thank you for all those who have given their lives because they loved you.

Didn't Saul, who looked after the coats, become famous?

He became Paul, didn't he?

That's right. Saul, who hunted Christians to kill them, became Paul, the great Christian missionary. He travelled thousands of miles telling people about Jesus. But that's another story. It's time we all went home. There's a lot to think about.

Boot whirred and the Livewires were caught up in a whirl of dust as he pulled them into his disk drive. As they whirled through the air, things seemed to become more and more familiar to them. The spinning stopped. The adventure was over and they tumbled down in a heap on the floor. They were back in Annie-log's bedroom, with Boot sitting quietly on the desk, just as if nothing had happened.

DIARY

SUNDAY
Did you manage to sort out what it is you might give to God? Have another think about it and try and plan what you are going to do.

MONDAY
There are some people we hear about often in the Bible, and others only once. They are all important to God.

TUESDAY
The freedmen came from Cyrene (a city in the country we now call Libya), Alexandria (an Egyptian sea port), Cilicia (a part of what is now Turkey: Paul was born in Tarsus, the chief city of Cilicia) and Asia.

WEDNESDAY
The Sanhedrin had seventy members and was led by the Chief Priest.

THURSDAY

Abraham	Joseph	Moses	David	Solomon	Jesus
1950 BC	1700 BC	1300 BC	1000 BC	950 BC	AD 1

BC means 'before Christ'. AD stands for Anno Domini—the year of our Lord. But Jesus was probably born in 4 BC—our calendar got it wrong!

FRIDAY
Paul became perhaps the greatest of all missionaries. Do you know any other missionaries? Can you find out if your church supports a missionary? If so, learn about what they do and where they work.

SATURDAY

> Lord Jesus, thank you for all those people who trust and believe in you. Help me to reach out to you in faith too, and to stretch right up in praise.

The Livewires were having a chat about their adventure.

Well, we certainly got about that time. Just amazing some of the places we've been and the people we've met.

It's the people I remember. David writing those beautiful Psalms. And giving me his harp.

And Solomon building the Temple.

And then Peter—I'll never forget Peter.

And meeting Mary after she had seen Jesus alive again.

You know what? It's much better THAN DOING IT AT SCHOOL! What do you think, Tempo?

Woof!

But where are all those people now? I mean, they lived on this earth, they loved Jesus and men like Stephen were even killed.

Surely they're in heaven with God?

I wonder what Boot has to say? Try him Annie-log.

Annie-log typed a few words onto Boot's keyboard, but he sat quietly on her desk. Nothing happened.

Look! I've found the story of Stephen in my Bible. It's in the book of Acts, chapter 7 verses 55 and 56.

Everyone gathered round.

Stephen looked up to heaven and saw God's glory and Jesus standing at the right hand side of God. *'Look!'* he said. *'I see heaven opened and the Son of Man standing at the right-hand side of God.'*

Heavenly Father, you are just that—my Father in heaven. Yet you care about me on earth. Thank you.

Can you unscramble what David sang about heaven right at the beginning of this book?

ROUYPRAISESEHCAER UPOTTHESNEVAEH

Who actually does the will of God in heaven?

Angels, I'm sure it's angels!

You don't believe in angels, do you?

I do. They bring bones!

But that's not all. The people who love Jesus go to heaven when they die.

Yes, people like Peter and Stephen and Mary. They will all be there.

But they were all a bit special—I mean, they were all part of the Bible story.

I think heaven's for ordinary people, who love Jesus, too. Let's ask Boot.

But once again Boot sat silently. Quartz was busy looking through her Bible.

Here we are! Matthew chapter 5 verse 12.

So it is for everyone—everyone who loves Jesus. Not just super saints and angels.

'Do not be worried and upset,' Jesus told them. 'Believe in God and believe also in me. There are many rooms in my Father's house and I am going to prepare a place for you. I would not tell you this if it were not so.'

Be happy and glad, for a great reward is kept for you in heaven.

Data pulled out her harp—it seemed to be a good moment to play it.

You might like to look this verse up in your own Bible. You'll find it in the New Testament. It's in the Gospel of John, chapter 14 verses 1–2.

62